Bloom for Yourself
JOURNAL

FOR THE CREATORS

love, april green

ISBN-9781694239617

This journal belongs to:

_____

If found, please return to:

_____

_____

_____

_____

Thank you.

love, april green

Contents:

I think that when you're entirely honest with yourself, a door opens within, and the light unfolds, and everything painful flies away.

Self-love is like a feeling you have to carry around with you for the rest of your life.

Like your beating heart: it should never stop.

And if you ever have one of those days when you feel like you're not enough, just become yourself—more passionately, more lovingly, and more intensely than ever before.

Sometimes,

(before you even know you need it)

your heart has already

given you the

answer.

It's okay if you're not yet
where you want to be.

Remember:

you don't always notice
the sun rising in the sky
until, one day, you feel
its warmth touching your face
and you realise how much
you have grown.

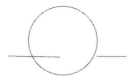

When you make a conscious choice
to be happy,
no-one can take it away from you
because no-one gave it to you:

you gave it to yourself.

Wildflower —

keep unfolding
in front of their eyes.

(without apology)

Healing is:

allowing flowers to grow
in all the places sadness
has touched inside you.

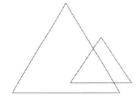

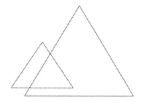

Sometimes, people come along
to show you the parts of yourself
you didn't know existed.

And when they leave —
you are altered:
you are braver, stronger
than ever before.

Keep close the ones

who believe in you.

To the ones

who feel too much:

make art.

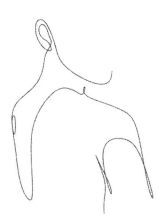

Love yourself enough
to recognise when your worth
is not valued the way it should
be.

Your breath has prayer in it,

and flowers, and rain, and salt
from the ocean's shifting tide.

I never think about the woman I was yesterday —
I have felt earth break beneath
      my knees with the soft fall of surrender.

I know that change is possible.

I affirm:

to fall in love with myself —
to hold all that I am
with fragile, thankful hands;
and know that I am holding a life,
a lesson, a future.

I create —

that's how I survive.

moment. by. moment.

Remember: it is your heart:

only you can nurture it;

only you can make it bloom.

You are allowed to leave
some pieces behind:

you are allowed to become
the person you design yourself
to be.

I believe very deeply
in the power you have
to build yourself back up.

You are your own light:

you do not need anyone else to
shine for you.

And the things we tell ourselves

can either destroy us or restore us.

(we write the story of our existence)

Let it go—

then see what kind of magic

returns in its place.

Because,

I promise that

what's for you

will never reach you

while you're clinging

to something else.

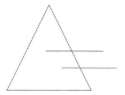

Some memories

never leave your bones.

Like salt in the sea,

they become part of you:

and you carry them.

love, april green

April Green is an author and advocate for change and growth. Her words are shared by thousands of people all over the world and are included in Jenna Dewan's debut book 'Gracefully You.'

All poetry and quotes in this journal are from the Bloom for Yourself books © April Green.

To read more of April's poetry and prose, follow her Instagram page: @loveaprilgreen.

For inspiration on journaling, follow her Instagram page: @bloomforyourself.

Books by April Green:

Bloom for Yourself
Bloom for Yourself II, Let go and Grow
Becoming a Wildflower.

Made in the USA
Columbia, SC
17 December 2019